THE HEYDAY OF THE
TRAM

PETER WALLER

First published 1992
Third impression 1996

ISBN 0 7110 2120 1

© Ian Allan Ltd 1992

Published by Ian Allan Publishing

an imprint of Ian Allan Ltd, Terminal House,
Station Approach, Shepperton, Surrey TW17 8AS
and printed by Ian Allan Printing Ltd,
Coombelands House, Addlestone, Surrey KT15 1HY

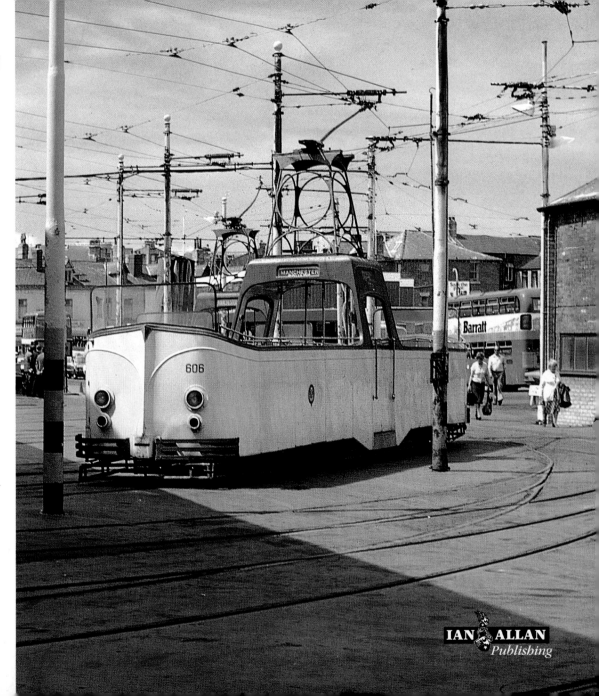

Front cover:
A typical street scene during the heyday of
trams in the British Isles: High Street, Dundee, is
portrayed in the early 1950s with, left to right,
No 29 of 1925, No 42 of 1920 and No 6 originally
dating from 1900. Roy Brook

Right:
Blackpool is now the only surviving electric
tramway in England. One of its unusual
open-top single-deck 'Boats', dating from 1934,
No 606 is seen at Rigby Road depot on 18 July
1981. Michael H. Waller

IAN ALLAN
Publishing

INTRODUCTION

The heyday of the tram is a difficult period to identify. In numerical terms the number of trams reached their peak, some 14,000, in the mid-1920s; but even by that stage a number of smaller systems had fallen by the wayside. Alternatively, the 1930s witnessed a considerable investment in new lines and vehicles by a number of important operators — most notably Sheffield, Liverpool, Leeds, Glasgow, Edinburgh and even London — whilst simultaneously the axe was wielded elsewhere. Even in 1945 there were almost 7,000 trams in operation in Britain and a large number of towns and cities had no well defined plans to abandon them.

1945 saw Britain's and Ireland's tramway systems in a number of conditions. There were those, like Manchester, which had been revived by the outbreak of war; there were those, like Blackpool and Leeds, where the tramcar represented the primary means of providing public transport and where the tramcar was still considered to be vitally important; there were those systems, predominantly in small towns like Gateshead, Dundee and Stockport, which had received little in the nature of modernisation but which seemed to be still wedded to the tramcar; and, finally, there were those lines, like the Great Orme, which were simply designed to cater for the tourist industry.

Inevitably, with the cessation of hostilities, those systems which had been threatened before the war were soon under threat again. Postwar austerity and the shortage of replacement vehicles undeniably delayed abandonment in a number of towns, but these conditions were not to prevail for ever. Gradually, but inevitably, these systems — Hull, Oldham, Plymouth, Darwen, South Shields, Manchester, Bolton, Bury, Bradford, Cardiff — disappeared. The enthusiast press could, and did, make a fuss over what it considered unnecessary closures, but years of under-investment and lack of maintenance could not be easily countered by the protestations of those who, at the time, were running against accepted orthodoxies.

For the supporters of the tram the greatest defeats were to come in those traditional strongholds of the tram — Liverpool, Glasgow, Leeds, Sheffield, Aberdeen, Edinburgh and even Blackpool — where the initial promise of the postwar years turned to abandonment. By 1962, and the final closure of the Glasgow system, the number of tramcars operational in Britain had declined to no more than a couple of hundred and the tram in its traditional, urban, environment was all but extinct.

Thirty years on, we can look back in hindsight and see that the abandonment of the tramcar was, in large measure, a serious mistake; the traffic problems allegedly caused by the tram remain — indeed have got a great deal worse. With the opening of the Manchester Metrolink project Britain has gained its first new street tramway for 40 years; the wheel has turned full circle in Manchester and, with other cities eager to follow, will no doubt turn elsewhere. Perhaps, in 50 years time the enthusiast of tomorrow will be able to look back and see the second half of the 1990s as the heyday of the tram.

Peter Waller,
Ashford,
June 1992

ACKNOWLEDGEMENTS

Three people in particular have been generous in allowing me access to their priceless collection of transparencies for the completion of this book. I am very grateful to Roy Brook, C. Carter and Geoff Lumb for their assistance; I doubt whether it would have proved possible to obtain such a variety of historic images without their help. I am also grateful to my good friend Paul Collins for verifying certain historical information.

ABERDEEN

Right:
The 'Granite City' of Aberdeen was one of four Scottish tramway systems to survive after 1945 and was the most northerly electric tramway in Britain (with the exception of the Cruden Bay line). It had survived into the postwar era relatively intact and was widely regarded, in the late 1940s and early 1950s, as one of the most secure tram operators in the country. A fleet of some 130 trams, some traditional and others more modern, operated over some eight routes. One of the last 'traditional' trams to be acquired No 124 (which was built in Aberdeen's own workshops in 1931) is pictured in St Nicholas Street operating on route No 7 to Woodside in August 1954. The Woodside route would be converted to bus operation on 26 November 1955, whilst car No 124 would survive until 1958.
Roy Brook

Left:
As with a number of other postwar operators, Aberdeen made use of second-hand tramcars to supplement its fleet at minimum cost. In 1936, 18 cars from Nottingham had been acquired (a 19th was acquired as a source of spares) and in 1948 the city took advantage of the gradual closure of Manchester's tramway system to acquire 14 of the 1930-32-built 'Pilcher' cars. One of the latter, No 39 (originally Manchester No 121), is seen in August 1954 on route No 4 to Hazlehead running along Castle Street. The Hazlehead route would survive for a further two years, being converted on 7 October 1956 and by the end of that year all of Aberdeen's 'Pilchers' would be withdrawn. *Roy Brook*

Above:
Aberdeen was also one of the tramway operators that acquired new trams in the immediate postwar years — new cars that seemed to bode well for the future of the system. In Aberdeen's case the new cars represented a batch of 20 centre-entrance streamlined cars, Nos 19-38, which were manufactured by Pickering in 1949. One of the class, No 34, is pictured in superb condition at the Hazlehead terminus of route No 4 in August 1955. Unfortunately, the promise that the new cars seemed to represent was illusory and the final Aberdeen tram route, the trunk route No 1 from Bridge of Don to Bridge of Dee, closed on 3 May 1958. All of the streamlined trams, indeed the whole Aberdeen fleet (efforts to preserve No 73 having come to nothing), went for scrap with the exception of one horse-tram. *Roy Brook*

BELFAST

Right:
The City of Belfast was Ireland's only standard gauge electric tramway (in reality it was, in fact, 4ft 9in) and was one of four tramways in Northern Ireland to survive into the postwar era. The system had grown through to the early 1930s but had seen significant closures both before and during the war with partial conversion to trolleybus operation. In August 1952, in the month prior to the route's closure, 'Moffett' class four-wheel car No 327 is pictured at the terminus of the route to Ballygomartin. The tram was one of a batch of 50, Nos 292-341, built by Brush and delivered between 1920 and 1921. Roy Brook

Below right:
The 50 'McCreary' cars delivered between 1935 and 1936 were the last new trams delivered to Belfast. Twenty of the class, Nos 392 and 423-441, were built by English Electric, whilst the remainder, Nos 393-422, were constructed locally by Service Motor Works. All were fitted with Maley & Taunton Swinglink trucks. One of the Service Motor Works cars, No 413, is seen at Ballygomartin in August 1952. The Belfast system finally closed on 28 February 1954 having died a long and lingering death. Of the Belfast fleet, two electric cars — converted horse car No 249 and 'Chamberlain' No 357 — are now displayed at the Belfast Transport Museum. Roy Brook

BIRMINGHAM

The Black Country, with Birmingham at its heart, formed the basis of the country's largest network of 3ft 6in gauge tramways. The biggest operator in the district, and the only one to survive into the postwar era, was Birmingham. A policy of abandonment had started prior to the outbreak of war in 1939, but this policy was suspended and was not resumed until March 1947. The city's first tramcars were a batch of 20 delivered by the Electric Railway & Tramway Carriage Works in 1904. Although 12 were destroyed by enemy action in 1941 the remaining eight cars survived until after 1945. Originally open-top, the trams had had top covers fitted prior to 1907 and platform vestibules were added between 1924 and 1929. One of the eight survivors, No 17 is pictured at Dale End on 9 July 1949.
C. Carter

Left:
Birmingham No 580 is pictured at Erdington, terminus of one of the city's last tram routes, in June 1953. The car was one of a batch of 75 introduced in 1913 and built by the United Electric Car Co Ltd. Originally the trams were fitted with Mountain & Gibson 'Burnley'-type bogies, but these were replaced with EMB bogies salvaged from cars destroyed during the Blitz. The Erdington route was converted to bus operation on 4 July 1953 along with the routes to Short Heath and Pype Hayes. Roy Brook

Left:
Running south of the city were a number of routes which ran along the Bristol Road reservation. One of these brought trams to the rural terminus at Rednal. This terminus was a popular destination on Sundays and holidays and led to the construction of both a conventional crossover terminus and a less common turning circle to accommodate the huge number of trams that were required to carry the passengers. When No 744 was photographed at the Rednal terminus in June 1952, shortly before the abandonment of the Bristol Road routes in July 1952, the loop was being used to accommodate stored trams. No 744 was one of a batch of 50 Brush-built trams constructed in 1928-29. Of Birmingham's 843 electric tramcars, only one, No 395 in the Birmingham Science Museum, survives. Roy Brook

BLACKBURN

The town of Blackburn was one of the more important 4ft 0in gauge operators of tramcars in Britain and formed, with Darwen and Accrington, a small narrow gauge system to the north of Manchester. Although two of Blackburn's routes had closed prior to the outbreak of World War 2, the remaining routes (including the through route to Darwen, despite the latter's persistent attempts to close the route) survived into the postwar era. After 1945 the elimination of the trams was soon reconfirmed as official policy and the first postwar closure occurred on 5 January 1946. Blackburn's trams were delivered in two batches in 1899 and 1900. The second batch, of 40 cars, were built by Milnes on Peckham 14B bogies. Although originally open-top, the majority were rebuilt with top covers between 1907 and 1935. Unlike Bradford, and many other narrow gauge systems, the rebuilt cars in Blackburn were fully enclosed. Car No 39 is pictured on the Intack route on 20 August 1949. C. Carter

Sister car, No 64, is also pictured on the Intack route. The Intack route, converted to bus operation on 3 September 1949, was Blackburn's final tram route. It was originally a short-working of the longer route to Church (which had been converted on 16 January 1949). Beyond Church, the route had joined the Accrington system and originally through trams had operated between the two towns. The location of Blackburn's depot at Intack no doubt influenced the, decision to keep this route to the end. None of Blackburn's fleet of tramcars survives in preservation. C. Carter

BLACKPOOL

In 1960 Blackpool celebrated the 75th anniversary of its electric tramway and four trams were specially restored for an anniversary procession held on 29 September of that year. Two of these were the surviving ex-conduit car of 1885 and the 'Dreadnought' car No 59. Car No 1 (it was in reality No 4) was originally built by Lancaster. On withdrawal in c1900 it had been converted to a works car, in which guise it continued to operate until final withdrawal in 1934. It was then stored until restoration for the 1960 celebrations; passing to the Tramway Museum Society and then returning to Blackpool for the centenary in 1985, when it was cosmetically restored as a conduit car and operated using battery power.

The 'Dreadnoughts' were designed to achieve rapid loading and unloading of passengers whilst operating on the busy promenade route. Some 20 'Dreadnoughts' were built between 1898 and 1902; the first were constructed as conduit cars, but these were quickly converted to overhead operation with the replacement of the original conduit route. All were withdrawn in 1934 but No 59, after considerable local pressure, was retained in store. Again, after restoration, the vehicle passed to the Tramway Museum Society. It returned to Blackpool on loan in 1976, but has since returned to Crich.

The Blackpool promenade tram route, promoted by Michael Holroyd Smith, was Britain's first electric tramway. After the many closures of the early 1960s, the route, which now runs from Starr Gate to Fleetwood, is Britain's only surviving conventional electric tramway.
Geoff Lumb

The Blackpool 'Standards' were the last traditional double-deck trams to operate on a British tramway. Between 1922 and 1929 more than 40 of the design were built. Although all bar three of the type survived into the postwar era, initially modernisation and later the contraction of the Blackpool tram system led to their eventual withdrawal. A number of 'Standards' survived the closure of the final 'town' routes in Blackpool (closed between 1961 and 1963) until the mid-1960s and this survival saw the type achieve great popularity. Consequently, the 'Standards' became popular vehicles for use on enthusiasts' tours. The last of the class were withdrawn during 1966 and, fortunately, no less than six have survived into preservation: two at the National Tramway Museum; one at Carlton Colville; and, three in the United States. One of the three now preserved in the USA, No 48, is seen on 28 October 1962 in Talbot Square — the last day of the Marton route. The tram is showing a fake 'Layton' destination; the Layton route having closed on 19 October 1936. Geoff Lumb

12

The Blackpool system, with its long promenade route, was always slightly atypical in its choice of tramcars. The 10 English Electric-built 'Pantograph' cars of 1928, Nos 167-176, were typical of the system's individuality. Also known as 'Pullmans' the cars were specifically designed for the route to Fleetwood. Originally fitted with pantographs — hence the name — the whole class had had replacement trolleypoles fitted in 1933. Of the 10, Nos 168-175 were further modernised between 1950 and 1953 by the replacement of their original McGuire bogies by English Electric bogies salvaged from Nos 10-21 (which were then being modernised to VAMBAC control for the Marton route). The first of the 10 was withdrawn for use as a test bed in 1950 and the remainder were withdrawn between 1954 and 1960. A couple were converted for use as works cars and one of these, No 167, passed to the Tramway Museum Society on final withdrawal in 1962. A number of others were used as the basis of some of Blackpool's famous illuminated trams. One of the cars fitted with replacement English Electric bogies, No 171, is seen heading north towards Little Bispham. Geoff Lumb

In the 1930s Blackpool, under the astute management of Walter Luff, undertook a dramatic modernisation of its tramcar fleet, acquiring, in the space of six years, more than 100 new tramcars. Amongst the last trams to be delivered were a batch of 20, Nos 284-303, delivered from Brush in 1937. Ironically, although Brush retained the capacity to manufacture tramcars into the 1950s, these trams were to be the last manufactured by the company. Eighteen of the class survived to be renumbered 621-38 in 1968 and although a number have subsequently been withdrawn, 13 remain in service. No 633, originally No 296, is seen at South Pier in 1975; sister car No 635 (No 298) has been preserved and is currently under restoration. Peter Waller

Although the majority of the trams acquired in the 1930s were single-deck, 27 of them were double-deck. Delivered in two batches from English Electric in 1934-35, the first 13 (Nos 237-49), which were open-top when new but which had top covers fitted during the war, were known as 'Luxury Dreadnoughts', whilst the remaining 14 (Nos 250-63) which were fully enclosed from new, were called 'Balloons'. Now numbered 700-26, the majority remain in service, although two formed the basis of the 'new' double-deck cars Nos 761/2 in 1979 and 1982. One of the type heads south in 1960. Geoff Lumb

Right:
In the late 1960s and early 1970s, Blackpool experimented with One Man Operation on the trams in an attempt to reduce operational costs, particularly in the winter. These experiments led, in 1972-76, to the construction of 13 OMO single-deck trams. These 13 were converted from 1930s-built streamlined railcoaches and were initially painted in a somewhat garish yellow and red livery. Subsequently, the trams were repainted red and cream, as exemplified by No 4 seen here at Starr Gate in 1975. With the introduction of the 'Centenary' class in 1985, the majority of the OMO cars have been withdrawn and one has been converted into a replica toastrack car. *Peter Waller*

Below right:
In 1984, following a period of considerable modernisation and improvement on Blackpool's surviving tram route, the first of a new batch of single-deck tramcars emerged. No 641, which was followed by seven further cars, was the result of co-operation between Blackpool Corporation and East Lancs coachbuilders and was the first tramcar to be manufactured by the firm. Inevitably called the 'Centenary' class, No 641 is appropriately captured in September 1985 during the actual centenary celebrations. *Michael H. Waller*

BOLTON

At its height Bolton formed an important part of the tram network north of Manchester, with links through to Bury and the independent operator South Lancashire Tramways. Closures in the prewar years had, however, reduced the network considerably and isolated the Bolton system. The tram's position in the town had been further undermined by the Ministry of War Transport's condemnation of two routes in 1944. These closures effectively left trams operating over five routes in the town in 1945. The majority of the town's trams had been acquired in the early years of the 20th century, with a limited amount of replacement in the 1920s. The last trams were, however, not acquired until 1943 when four second-hand cars were acquired from Bury. None of the fleet was preserved when the Bolton system closed in March 1947, but a number of bodies did survive and one of these, No 66, a car built originally in 1901-02 by the Electric Railway & Tramway Carriage Works on Brill 21E bogies, was rescued and restored. It is seen here running on a special tour of Blackpool, its current home, on 18 July 1981. Bolton used route letters rather than numbers and route 'E' was used for cars on the route to Deane. Peter Waller

BOURNEMOUTH

On the closure of the 3ft 6in gauge system in the south coast resort of Bournemouth in 1936, 10 of the system's open-top double-deck trams were acquired by the Llandudno & Colwyn Bay Electric Railway in North Wales. In their new home, the 10 trams were destined to give a further two decades of service before the L&CBER also closed. Of the 10 trams sent north, nine had been originally built between 1921 and 1926, whilst the 10th was older, having been constructed in 1914. Numbered 7-16 and 6 respectively by the L&CBER, it was No 6 that was to become the official last tram when the L&CBER closed on 24 March 1956. The UEC-built car was then acquired for preservation and, after a period of display at the Museum of British Transport at Clapham, it returned to its home town. Now restored as Bournemouth No 85 the tram is displayed at Mallard Road depot. *Peter Waller*

BRADFORD

The biggest operator of 4ft 0in gauge trams in Britain was the city of Bradford. Although a steady conversion programme to both trolleybus and motorbus had started in the late 1920s, the city still possessed a network of seven routes and some 90 trams in 1945. During the war, it is believed due to the influence of vehicles from Southend on loan, the city's mixed fleet of bus, trolley and tram received a light blue livery in place of the Prussian blue of prewar years. No 107, a product of the corporation's Thornbury Works in 1920, is seen in the postwar livery at Queensbury, the terminus of the highest tram route in Britain.
C. Carter

When the Bradford tramway system closed on 6 May 1950 it brought the story of the British 4ft 0in gauge tram to an end — almost. Although none of the Bradford trams were initially preserved, the city's last tramcar No 104, one of a fleet of identical English Electric tramcars built between 1921 and 1930, became a scoreboard at the famous Odsal Rugby League ground. It remained grounded for several years until the efforts of local enthusiasts saw the body recovered and the tram restored to operational condition. The original truck had been scrapped but a replacement — albeit not from one of the Bradford trams sold to the city — was obtained from Sheffield. Fully restored in the prewar Prussian blue, the tram operated for a number of years within the precincts of Thornbury depot — the first tramcar to be restored, phoenix-like, from the dead. It is seen here, on 7 May 1960, on one of its occasional forays. After the mid-1960s the tram was stored in Thornbury depot until it was transferred to the new Bradford Industrial Museum in the mid-1970s where it can now be viewed. Geoff Lumb

DOUGLAS

The horse tramway in the Manx capital of Douglas is one of the three surviving tramways on this small island and is the only surviving horse tramway in the British Isles. The first section of line opened in 1876 and, despite plans for its electrification, has been horse operated throughout its history. Although the number of operational trams has declined from the 46 that survived into the postwar era, there are still some 20 available to provide this popular service along the town's promenade. One of the many open toastracks heads south on 19 July 1964, viewed from a northbound car. *Geoff Lumb*

DUNDEE

Dundee was the smallest of the four Scottish tramway operators to survive into the postwar era and was, in many ways, the last wholly traditional tramway to close. The system comprised some 60 passenger trams and some five radiating routes in 1945. By 1950, of the surviving 56 trams, the newest cars had been delivered in 1930 and the oldest were already 50 years old. Although Dundee made efforts to acquire either new or second-hand trams, it proved impractical to obtain such additional vehicles — due in part to the system's adoption of the minimum space (3ft 6in) between the parallel running lines, which precluded the use of conventional width tramcars. In August 1955 one of the original batch of 1900-built trams, No 6, is pictured at the terminus of the Downfield route. These 10 cars, which had been much modified in the 55-year life, were destined to be withdrawn in 1955 upon the suspension of the Blackness-Downfield route. The route was 'temporarily' converted to bus operation on 26 November 1955, as part of a year's experiment, but was destined never to be operated by trams again.

Right:
One of a batch of eight delivered in 1902, No 18, seen here on the Lochee route in August 1954, was originally an open-top bogie car built by Milnes. All eight cars were rebuilt as fully enclosed four-wheelers between 1928 and 1930. As with the cars of batch Nos 1-10, the suspension of the Blackness-Downfield route allowed for these trams to be withdrawn. Both Roy Brook

The newest trams operated in Dundee were the 10 'Lochee' cars acquired in 1930. These cars were slightly wider than the normal Dundee tram and were, therefore, normally limited to operation on the Lochee route, where the separation between the running tracks was greater. Elsewhere, although a single 'Lochee' car could operate safely, two 'Lochee' cars could not pass. One of the type, No 27, is pictured at Lochee terminus in August 1955. By the mid-1950s, although Dundee's maintenance ensured that the trams remained in excellent condition, advertising had started to appear. The last routes in Dundee, to Lochee and Ninewells-Maryfield, were converted to bus operation on 20 October 1956. Although two trams, including a 'Lochee' car, were offered for preservation, it proved impractical and all Dundee's surviving trams were scrapped. Roy Brook

EDINBURGH

The Scottish capital city of Edinburgh was a relatively late user of electric tramcars: the city's fleet of cable cars only passing into municipal ownership in 1919. Initially, many of the cable cars inherited were converted to electric traction, but gradually these were replaced by new electric trams. The process of building new trams continued until 1950 — six years before the system was finally abandoned. No 11, built by Hurst Nelson in 1935, is seen heading for Foot of Leith Walk in 1953. No 11 was to survive in service until July 1956 — four months prior to the final closure. Roy Brook

Edinburgh 214 was one of three trams delivered to the city in 1940 and was built in the corporation's own workshops at Shrubhill as part of the continuing programme of replacing the converted cable cars. It is seen in August 1955 running along Princes Street, a year before withdrawal, on route No 13 to Churchill. The Churchill/Granton circular, routes Nos 13 and 14, would be converted to bus operation on 17 June 1956. The tracks along Princes Street were one of the weaknesses of the Edinburgh system, particularly after the parallel tracks in George Street were abandoned, since Princes Street was regularly closed to traffic for official processions. Of Edinburgh's fleet of electric trams only one, No 35 built in 1948 and similar to No 214, survives. Roy Brook

GATESHEAD

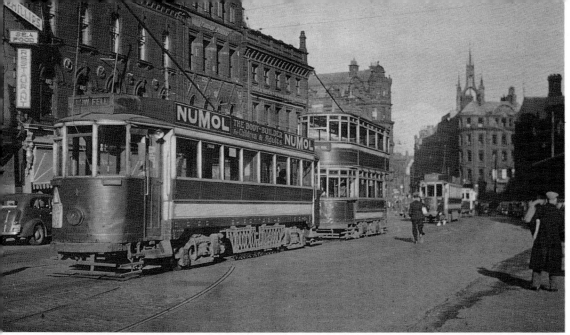

Above left:
One of the most important promoters of tramways in Britain was British Electric Traction (BET), but by 1945 its once large empire had contracted to the solitary system of Gateshead. Initially separate from its larger neighbour across the Tyne, Newcastle, the two systems were linked by two bridges constructed during the 1920s and a number of through routes were introduced. Inevitably, the history of the twin systems became intertwined, particularly after Newcastle adopted the trolleybus as a tram replacement and sought to persuade Gateshead to follow suit. Although constantly threatened, Gateshead acquired a number of additional second-hand trams during the immediate postwar period but was unable to prevent ultimately the tide of abandonment. The Gateshead system, with many low bridges, saw the operation of numerous single-deck trams. One of these, No 4 (one of a batch of 20 built between 1920 and 1928) is seen at Newcastle Central station on 21 September 1950. At this time all Newcastle trams had been withdrawn, leaving Gateshead as the sole operator across the Tyne. On withdrawal in Gateshead, 14 of the batch, including No 4, were sold to the Grimsby & Immingham line; two of these, Nos 5 and 10, have been preserved. C. Carter

Below left:
Apart from the fleet of single-deck trams, Gateshead also operated a number of double-deck vehicles. Some of these had been new to the system, others had been acquired second-hand from Liverpool (via Tynemouth & District) or Sheffield during the mid-1920s. The majority had originally been open-top and had been rebuilt with top covers and platform vestibules. Further second-hand double-deck cars came postwar from Oldham. One of the open balcony double-deck cars, No 32 (originally built in 1901 and rebuilt during the 1920s), is seen at Heworth on 17 May 1949; the magnet and wheel symbol of BET can be clearly seen on the side of the car. The final Gateshead trams operated on 4 August 1951; although Newcastle had abandoned its last trams in March the previous year, Gateshead continued to operate into Newcastle until final closure. C. Carter

GLASGOW

Above
The city of Glasgow possessed the second largest tramway in the British Isles and, in the postwar years, the biggest. It also adopted the unusual gauge, like Huddersfield, of 4ft 7¾in. It was also unusual in that it perpetuated the tradition of route colours much longer than elsewhere. 'Standard' No 698, when photographed on Argyle Street on 22 June 1951, wears blue; other colours used included red and white. The route colours gradually disappeared by the early 1950s. Built in 1899, No 698 would be

withdrawn in 1952 at a time when serious inroads were being made into the fleet of 'Standards' with the introduction of the 'Cunarders' and the first route withdrawals. C. Carter

Right:
The Glasgow 'Standards' were the second most numerous design of tramcar in Britain, with over 1,000 being constructed over a 25-year period. No 665 was the second 'Standard' to bear that particular number (and the third Glasgow tram in all) and was built in 1923. The original 'Standard' No 665 was scrapped before World War 1. If the original plans to construct 600

'Coronation' cars had been fulfilled then the lifetime of the 'Standards' would have been considerably shortened. As it was, the failure to complete the 'Coronation' programme and the exigencies caused by World War 2 gave the 'Standards' a much longer life than originally intended. It was the increasing age and condition of the 'Standards' in the early 1950s that was one factor in the initial Glasgow abandonment scheme. No 665, pictured here at Maryhill depot, was one of the last 'Standards' to be withdrawn, succumbing in November 1960. Five 'Standards' have been preserved, including two at the National Tramway Museum. Geoff Lumb

Left:
By the early 1960s the Glasgow network had shrunk dramatically and by the end of 1961 only three routes remained operational. The first of these to close was route No 15 on 10 March 1962. On 2 June 1962 the penultimate route, No 26 from Clydebank to Dalmarnock, was converted leaving only route No 9 to continue to the final closure. On 21 April 1962 'Coronation' No 1249, one of a class of 150 built from 1936 to 1941, runs over route No 26. Itself built in 1939, No 1249 was to survive the closure of route No 26 by only a few days, being withdrawn on 18 June 1962, almost exactly 23 years after it had entered service; it had received a new top deck after suffering fire damage in 1953. *Geoff Lumb*

Above:
Glasgow's last tram route, No 9 from Dalmuir West to Auchenshuggle, was withdrawn on 4 September 1962 — making Glasgow the last complete system to close in the British Isles. A 'Coronation' car traverses Argyle Street, then retaining but a shadow of its former importance as a tram thoroughfare, having just passed underneath the ex-LMS Central station. Inevitably, a number of Glasgow trams survive in preservation, and this includes four of the 'Coronation' class. *Geoff Lumb*

GREAT ORME

Running in two sections up to the summit of Great Orme, the Great Orme Tramway is neither a conventional electric tramway (despite the presence of overhead) nor a cable tramway; it is rather a long funicular where the ascending car is assisted by the descent of its twin. The 3ft 6in gauge line was opened in two stages in 1902 and 1903 and, despite almost failing in the 1930s due to a fatal accident, continues to operate to the present day. Two cars operate each section: Nos 4 and 5 on the lower section and 6 and 7 on the upper. All four cars were built by Hurst Nelson in 1902 and 1903 and the original cars remain in service. No 7 is seen departing from Half Way, where the two sections meet. The overhead was used for communications when this photograph was taken; with the installation of radio equipment the retention of the overhead is now purely cosmetic.
Geoff Lumb

GRIMSBY & IMMINGHAM

The Grimsby & Immingham was originally constructed by the Great Central Railway to bring workers from Grimsby to work in the newly-constructed docks at Immingham. Between 1911 and 1915 Brush supplied 16 single-deck tramcars to operate the line. Of these 16, three had been withdrawn before the outbreak of World War 2 but the remaining cars survived into the 1950s and some to the line's closure in 1961. After the Grouping the line passed to the London & North Eastern Railway (one of two tramways operated by the LNER) and then after 1948 to British Railways. The last of the Brush-built cars, No 16, is seen operating towards Immingham. The tram is seen in the BR standard all-over green livery adopted in 1951 for electric rolling stock. After closure, one of the Brush-built cars, No 14, was secured for preservation. It is now displayed at the National Tramway Museum.
Geoff Lumb

By the early 1950s the existing Grimsby & Immingham fleet was becoming both life-expired and incapable of handling the additional traffic caused by the development of industrial plants alongside the line. Three cars had already been acquired from Newcastle when, in 1951, the decision was made to buy 19 single-deck trams from Gateshead. These new acquisitions allowed for the withdrawal of the ex-Newcastle trams and the gradual elimination of some of the original Brush-built trams. Of the 19 trams acquired, 17 entered service (Nos 17-33) and one was destroyed in transit. The 19th, ex-Gateshead No 17, was converted for use as a works car and numbered DE320224. This last car is seen at Pyewipe depot. By the late 1950s British Railways were finding the costs of operating the Grimsby & Immingham increasingly burdensome, particularly as no support was forthcoming from those other industries along the line whose staff made use of the service, and consequently, after much controversy, the line finally closed on 1 July 1961. Geoff Lumb

HILL OF HOWTH

Left:
The Great Northern Railway (Ireland) owned two tramways. One was the Fintona horse tramway, north of the border, and the second was the 5ft 3in gauge Hill of Howth line near Dublin. The line opened in two stages in 1901 and, in order to operate the initial services, eight open-top double-deck trams, Nos 1-8, were acquired from Brush. For its entire history the Hill of Howth line was primarily a tourist service carrying passengers to the 560ft summit, but by the early 1950s the financial position of the parent GNR(I) and the successor Great Northern Railway Board was in serious decline and this led to threats to the survival of the route. Closure notices first appeared in 1954, but the proposed closure caused much controversy and the line was temporarily reprieved. Final closure was, however, to come on 31 May 1959. With the demise of the Howth line the history of the tram in Ireland came to a close. In happier times, Brush-built car No 1 ascends to the Summit in the blue and white livery of the GNR(I) during August 1952. Roy Brook

Right:
Apart from the eight Brush-built trams of 1901, the Hill of Howth line acquired two further passenger cars in 1902 — Nos 9 and 10. These Milnes-built cars were unusual in that they ran in a teak livery rather than the GNR(I)'s usual blue and white. No 10 is seen outside Sutton depot in August 1956. After the line's closure No 9 was preserved in Dublin, whilst No 10 passed to the Tramway Museum Society and was regauged for preservation in Britain. Fully restored the car took part in the Blackpool centenary celebrations of 1985. Sutton depot continued in use after the demolition of the tramway as a store for withdrawn steam engines and for departmental use by CIE. Roy Brook

LEEDS

Left:

In 1931-32 Leeds introduced a class of 100 four-wheeled cars to the design of the then General Manager R. L. Horsfield. The cars, unlike the five prototype trams which had been built by Brush (Nos 150-154), were manufactured in the Corporation's own works at Kirkstall Road. Numbered 155-254, the class was known as either 'Showboats' or 'Horsfields'. The class was destined to remain in service until 1956-59 and, with the 'Felthams', were the last Leeds trams to remain in service. No 165 is seen at the Corn Exchange on 22 September 1950 on route No 8 to Elland Road. The route, which originally went beyond Elland Road to Morley, was converted to bus operation on 25 June 1955, but received a temporary reprieve in 1956 as a result of the Suez crisis. The tram is in the blue livery which was destined to be replaced from May 1950 by a predominantly red colour scheme. C. Carter

Above:

Amongst the most stylish tramcars ever built in Britain were the 17 bogie cars delivered between 1933 and 1935 for use on the Middleton Light Railway. Built by Brush and English Electric, one of the eight built by the later company, No 268, is seen operating on route No 26 to Middleton in Meadow Lane on 22 September 1950. At this time, the final extension to the Middleton route had just been opened, completing the circular route. This extension was one of relatively few to be built in Britain after 1945; the Middleton route was to be converted to bus operation on 28 March 1959. The route was to outlive the 'Middleton bogies' by some two years; unfortunately, none of the type were to be preserved. C. Carter

Just prior to the outbreak of World War 2, Leeds bought three 'HR/2' cars from the London Passenger Transport Board. Built by English Electric in 1931, the cars were only eight years old when sold to Leeds. Numbered 277-79 in Leeds, the three were destined to last for 18 years in their northern home. The first of the three, No 277 (originally LPTB No 1881), is seen operating on the Lawnswood route — one of the most prestigious routes in Leeds — in 1949. The third of the class, No 279, was to become the last Leeds tram to operate in the blue livery. Although none of the Leeds trio survives, one 'HR/2', No 1858, is displayed at the East Anglian Transport Museum. C. Carter

In 1943 Leeds Corporation built an Austerity replacement double-deck tram to cover for the loss of one of the 1926-27-built 'Pivotal' cars. No 104, as it was then numbered, was constructed in the corporation's own workshops at Kirkstall and was fitted with a Peckham P35 truck. It was destined to be the penultimate new double-deck tramcar built for Leeds — apart from No 276 all future double-deck purchases would be second-hand. It was renumbered 275 in 1948 and is seen at the Half Mile Lane terminus of the Stanningley route, with the conductor about to reverse the bow collector, in 1952. The section from Half Mile Lane to Stanningley was one of the first significant postwar conversions, being abandoned on 2 January 1953. No 275 was to survive until 1957. *Roy Brook*

Leeds was a second place to obtain 'Pilcher' trams that were surplus to requirements in Manchester. A total of seven were bought between 1946 and 1948. No 285, originally Manchester No 263, is seen at Low Road, Hunslet, in c1952. With the arrival of the first ex-London Transport 'Felthams' and the start of the abandonment policy, the 'Pilchers' were destined to have a relatively short life in Leeds, being withdrawn between 1952 and 1954. Roy Brook

The 20 'Beeston Air Brakes' were built by Leeds Corporation between 1925 and 1928. They were the first trams that Leeds possessed to be fitted with air brakes. When seen in c1952 at Abbey Road, Kirkstall, No 396 retained the blue livery that was at that time being phased out. By this stage the only trams that retained the blue livery were largely those, like the 'Beeston Air Brakes', destined for early withdrawal. The last of the class was withdrawn in 1954, although one, No 399, survived, after a period in use as a works car, to be preserved. The passenger service to Kirkstall — the remains of a much longer route through Hawksworth Road to Guiseley — was converted to bus operation on 3 April 1954, although access was retained to Kirkstall works until 1957. Roy Brook

Right:
One of the popular 'Horsfield' class, No 191, is pictured on the private right of way which served the route to Temple Newsam. The three routes along the York Road — to Halton, Cross Gates and Temple Newsam — were the last three routes to be served by trams in Leeds and finally were converted on 7 November 1959. Sister car, No 160, acted as the official last car; of the 'Horsfields' one, No 180, survives in the collection of the National Tramway Museum.
Geoff Lumb

Far right:
In an effort to modernise their trams systems the Metropolitan Electric Tramways and the London United Tramways acquired 100 bogie trams from the Union Construction & Finance Co of Feltham in 1931. Known, inevitably, as the 'Felthams', the 100 cars passed to the London Passenger Transport Board in 1933 and were renumbered 2066-2165 by the LPTB. Transferred away from their traditional haunts as a result of the pre-World War 2 conversions, all bar two of the class survived into the postwar era operating over the surviving south London tram routes. Withdrawals, however, proceeded swiftly during the final conversion of the London tramway system — 'Operation Tramaway' — in 1950-52. Ninety of the trams were to be given a second life through being sold to Leeds. Whilst not all entered service in the Yorkshire city, the majority were to give several years of further operation. One of the ex-MET 'Felthams', now renumbered 525 by Leeds, awaits departure from the terminus at Cross Gates. Two of the ex-MET 'Felthams' survive: one in the London Transport Museum and the second in the United States of America. One of the ex-LUT cars was also preserved but, unfortunately, was eventually scrapped after suffering vandalism whilst stored on the Middleton Railway. *Geoff Lumb*

LEICESTER

Right:
The town of Leicester was, by 1945, the last surviving tram operator in the East Midlands. Although a number of routes had closed prior to 1939, the system retained 13 routes radiating out from the town operated by some 160 virtually identical four-wheel cars. No 68, one of a batch of 99 open-top cars delivered between 1903 and 1905 is seen on the East Park Road route. All bar four trams of this batch were rebuilt as fully enclosed and one, No 76, survives in preservation at the National Tramway Museum. The East Park Road route was converted to bus operation on 15 May 1949. C. Carter

Below right:
The first postwar closure in Leicester occurred on 2 May 1945 when the Welford Road route was converted to bus operation. There was then a 20-month gap before the next conversion in January 1947. Thereafter Leicester's trams were converted over a three-year period, with the last conversion taking place on 9 November 1949. No 138, a United Electric Car Co Ltd product of 1905, is seen on the Blackbird Road route, which was one of eight routes to be converted to bus operation during 1949. C. Carter

LIVERPOOL

Far right:
Liverpool No 637, one of many 'Priestly' cars built in the 1920s, is seen at Pier Head on 15 May 1950. The Pier Head, with its three loops, was one of the most complex tramway termini in the country. The majority of the 'Priestly' cars were built in Liverpool's own workshops and, by the introduction of this batch in 1924, were fitted with closed top-deck balconies although the lower-deck vestibules remained open. Modernisation saw most of the cars completely enclosed. The 'Priestly' cars were progressively withdrawn between 1946 and 1952 as the conversion programme in Liverpool gradually took effect. C. Carter

Right:
Of all Britain's tramway systems, Liverpool, with its huge investment in segregated tram reservations and in some 300 new streamlined trams between 1935 and 1942, was the most ideally placed to see the tramcar survive in the urban environment. Despite these advantages, Liverpool was to abandon its trams in a 10-year programme from 1948-57. One of the modern streamlined four-wheel trams, No 182, is pictured at Kirkby in August 1954. The extension along the East Lancs Road to Kirkby was opened in a number of stages through to April 1944, although the final stretch — Liverpool's last extension — was destined to be used only at peak hours. Route No 19 to Kirkby was converted to bus operation in November 1956. *Roy Brook*

Far right:
The streamline four-wheel cars were nicknamed 'Baby Grands' and here No 203 is seen at Page Moss on route No 40 in July 1956. Route No 40 to Page Moss was one of the last two tram routes to operate in Liverpool, being converted to bus operation on 14 September 1957. One of the 'Baby Grands' No 293 (now preserved in the United States) was the official last car, whilst a second, No 245, is preserved in Liverpool. *Roy Brook*

The bogie version of the 'Baby Grand' was known as the 'Green Goddess' and, like the four-wheel model, first appeared in the mid-1930s. No 990 is seen at Page Moss on route No 40 in August 1954. After withdrawal a number of the 'Green Goddesses', but not No 990, were sold to Glasgow. One of the sold cars, No 869 (Glasgow No 1055), was subsequently preserved and is now displayed at Crich. Roy Brook

LLANDUDNO & COLWYN BAY

The Llandudno & Colwyn Bay Electric Railway in North Wales, was the last narrow gauge (3ft 6in) tramway to close in Britain. Dating originally from 1907, the line had seen considerable modernisation in the 1930s with the acquisition of second-hand trams from Accrington and Bournemouth. One of the ex-Accrington single-deck trams, No 2, is seen during the summer of 1954. The ex-Accrington cars had to be regauged before they could run over the L&CBER. Roy Brook

49

In 1936, 10 open-top double-deck trams were acquired from Bournemouth for passenger service; an 11th was also acquired for works' duties. Of the 10, nine were built by Brush in the 1920s with Brill 22E bogies. One of the Brush-built cars, No 8, is seen at West Shore. The Llandudno & Colwyn Bay Electric Railway closed, despite efforts to preserve it, on 24 March 1956. One of the Bournemouth cars, No 6, acted as the official last tram and was subsequently preserved. Roy Brook

LONDON

With the entrance to Blackwall Tunnel in the background, ex-LCC 'HR/2' type No 147 prepares to depart to Victoria. When formed in 1933 the London Passenger Transport Board inherited Britain's largest tramway network. Prewar closures of most of the network north of the Thames had led to the transfer of relatively recent cars south of the river. The war intervened and delayed the final closure of London's tramway network. It was only in 1950 that the process of final abandonment — Operation Tramaway — commenced, with London's last trams operating on 6 July 1952. Route No 58 was to be converted to bus operation during Stage 5 of the conversion programme, on 6/7 October 1951.
C. Carter

Far left:
Another Corporation fleet to be inherited by the LPTB was that of West Ham. Here ex-West Ham No 344 is seen operating on route No 36 Abbey Wood-Embankment. Although the majority of London's surviving tramway network after World War 2 was conduit, there were significant stretches of overhead as well, which led to the famous institution of the change-pit, where trams were converted from overhead to conduit or vice versa. The existence of the trolleybus overhead is a reminder that London also possessed Britain's largest trolleybus network. C. Carter

Left:
The largest element within the LPTB tram network was formed by the lines and vehicles inherited from the erstwhile London County Council. In 1930-31 the LCC introduced a batch of 100 'E/3s' built in its own workshops on EMB maximum-traction bogies. One of these, No 1931, is pictured on route No 46, which linked Woolwich and Southwark Bridge. Route No 46, along with No 36 pictured earlier, was one of six routes to survive through until the closure of London's trams in July 1952. C. Carter

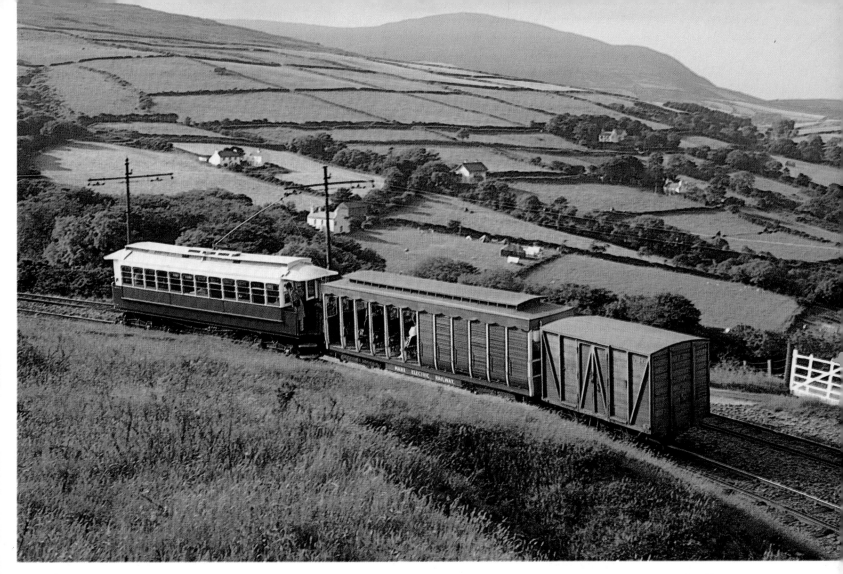

MANX ELECTRIC RAILWAY

The Manx Electric Railway, the second of the three surviving tramways on the Isle of Man, is , at 17 miles in length, the longest of all Britain's remaining tramways. The first section of the line, from Douglas to Groudle Glen, opened in 1893 and further extensions saw the line completed to Ramsey in 1899. Unusual in Britain, *in that it saw both trailer and mixed-traffic operation, the line has survived despite being buffeted by both financial hardship and the stormy seas. A train, headed by one of the original two power cars (built by Milnes in 1893) with a cross bench trailer and covered wagon, heads north on 22 July 1964. Geoff Lumb*

1899-built power car No 20 heads a crossbench trailer over a level crossing on a southbound working on 22 July 1964. The Manx Electric is built to the Isle of Man standard gauge of 3ft. A similar car, No 22, was destroyed by fire in the depot at Douglas in September 1990, but has been completely rebuilt as original. The 'new' car was unveiled in early 1992. Geoff Lumb

ROTHERHAM

Of all the British tramways to survive after 1945 the most unusual was possibly the single route at Rotherham. Although the bulk of the Rotherham system had been abandoned before the war, the unwillingness of Sheffield to replace the trams on the through route between the two towns led Rotherham to invest in 11 single-ended trams for use over the route in 1934 and 1935. One of the English Electric-built cars, No 9, is seen at the reversing point at Templeborough, on the borough boundary. The through service was suspended in 1948 due to the need to replace a bridge at Tinsley and was never reinstated. With their sole raison d'être having disappeared, it was not long before the final Rotherham tram operated. The last day was 13 November 1949 and all of Rotherham's surviving trams, including the single-ended cars, were scrapped. C. Carter

SHEFFIELD

Sheffield was the last city in England to abandon its tramway system; the compact network, worked entirely by four-wheel cars, finally closing on 8 October 1960 — a sad end to one of Britain's most attractive and modern systems. One of the most familiar landmarks in the city is the Wicker Arch, which carried the former Great Central main line over the Wicker (one of the busiest roads in the city). A total of seven tram routes used this particular thoroughfare, and No 183, one of a batch of 40 cars built by the Corporation itself in 1933-34, heads north towards the terminus at Vulcan Road. The route from Vulcan Road/Weedon Street to Beauchief/Millhouses was destined to become the last converted to bus operation in the city. One of this batch of cars, No 189, survives at the National Tramway Museum. Geoff Lumb

Built in 1935 on Peckham P22 trucks, the 29 cars of batch Nos 202-30 were the last of this particular design to emerge. The first flush-sided, rather than the tradition rocker panel design, tram in Sheffield had appeared in 1927 and more than 130 similar cars were constructed between then and 1934. The majority of these, like No 230 — the last of all — were built in the Corporation's own workshops at Queens Road. No 230 is seen at the terminus of the Beauchief route in the late summer of 1959. Geoff Lumb

Above:
The next stage in the development of the
Sheffield tram was the so-called 'domed roof'
design, which first appeared in 1936. A total of
67 of this design were built between then and
the outbreak of war in 1939. A further 14 similar
cars were built between 1941 and 1944 to
replace trams destroyed during the enemy
bombing of the city; these 14 cars taking the
numbers of the cars previously destroyed. One
of the wartime replacement cars, No 430, is seen
on the Wadsley Bridge via Queens Road service
running along Abbey Lane. The Wadsley Bridge

route was converted to bus operation on
3 October 1959. No 430 was to last longer, being
amongst those trams withdrawn with the final
closure of the system in October 1960. One of the
original domed-roof cars, No 264, is displayed at
the National Tramway Museum.
Geoff Lumb

Right:
In the post-1945 era the emergence of a new
tramcar manufacturer was unusual and
Charles Roberts & Co was one of the few. The

largest batch of trams built by this firm were the
35 four-wheel cars, Nos 502-36, delivered to
Sheffield between 1950 and 1952. No 523 is seen
at Heeley, using the crossover prior to departure
for Pitsmoor. By the time the final 'Roberts' cars
were delivered the fateful decision to abandon
Sheffield's trams had been taken, and the cars
were to have a life of less than a decade. Two of
the type, Nos 510 and 513 (both of which were
used in the closure procession), have been
preserved. Geoff Lumb

SNAEFELL

Left:
One of the six Snaefell Mountain Railway trams, No 3, is seen descending the mountain in 1960. The Snaefell line was built to the unusual gauge — for the Isle of Man — of 3ft 6in. The island's standard gauge is 3ft, but the extra 6in were required to accommodate the Fell centre rail. This extra rail is used primarily for braking on the steeper sections. The line, which has always been associated with the Manx Electric (which it meets at Laxey), opened in 1895 and is one of three tramways to survive to the modern day on the Isle of Man. The unusual twin pantographs are original and based upon a patent lodged by John Hopkinson, who supervised the installation of the line's electrical equipment. Originally the power cars of the MER were similarly fitted, but they were subsequently fitted with conventional trolleypoles. Five of the original Milnes-built cars survive; the sixth was destroyed by fire in 1971 and subsequently rebuilt. *Geoff Lumb*

Above:
For a brief period the cars of the Snaefell Mountain Railway were painted in green and white. One car, so painted, is seen with the Air Ministry radar station in the background during 1960. It was the construction of the radar station that brought much unseasonal traffic to the line in the early 1950s; normally, being a tourist attraction alone, the Snaefell line operates only during the holiday season. Geoff Lumb

SOUTHAMPTON

Southampton possessed one of the last tramway systems along the south coast of England and could also lay claim as the place where the private preservation of trams, which culminated in the creation of the National Tramway Museum at Crich, started. The profile of Southampton's fleet of enclosed trams — such as 1928-built No 37 pictured here en route for Shirley — was due to the Bargate — the mediaeval entry to the city through which the trams had to pass. The Bargate was only bypassed in the 1930s, by which stage Southampton's trams were soon to start to disappear. The war intervened to ensure a longer life than anticipated, but the final routes were converted on 31 December 1949. A number of the fully-enclosed trams, such as No 37, were sold to Leeds, but not all entered service in Yorkshire. The sorry state of the car merits comment; it was the presence of certain older, open-top knifeboard trams seen during an otherwise depressing tour of August 1948, that led to the preservation of Southampton No 45 — the first privately preserved tram. C. Carter

STOCKPORT

Situated to the south of Manchester, the small system of Stockport was, paradoxically, one of the few places in 1945 that was not actively considering the abandonment of its trams — indeed the transport press at that time were confidently expecting the imminent relaying of the complex junction at Mersey Square. However, the continuing abandonment programme in neighbouring Manchester — with whom Stockport shared a number of joint routes — made it impossible for Stockport to stand against the tide and a policy of abandonment was instituted in 1949. The last Stockport tram ran on 25 August 1951. One of Stockport's typical four-wheel fully-enclosed cars, No 56, one of a batch of 10 built by English Electric in 1920, loads with passengers in Mersey Square — the hub of the Stockport system — on 21 August 1949. C. Carter

SUNDERLAND

Far left:
Sunderland was one of four tram operators in northeast England to survive into the post-1945 era and was destined to become the longest lived. It was, in many ways, a peculiar system: it opened one of the relatively few postwar extensions; it used pantographs rather than the more widely used trolley pole or bow collector; and, finally, it had a curious assortment of new and second-hand trams. Of its fleet of around 90 trams some 30 had their origins in systems stretching from South Shields in the north to Portsmouth in the south — including two from Accrington which had to be regauged before use on the northeast coast! Truly, Sunderland was a tram lover's mecca.

In 1937-38 Sunderland acquired eight trams, numbered 2-9, from the LPTB. These trams, dating from 1932, had originally been delivered to Ilford Corporation and were rendered surplus to requirements in the Metropolis by the prewar conversion scheme. The first of the type, No 2 (originally Ilford No 33), is pictured on 1 October 1954 at the Seaburn terminus on the last day of Sunderland's tramway operations. The ex-Ilford cars were originally fitted with Peckham P22 trucks, but these were replaced in 1946-48 by Maley & Taunton Hornless trucks. Roy Brook

Left:
Another source of second-hand tramcars was Huddersfield, whose batch of eight 1931 English Electric-built trams (Nos 137-144) passed to Sunderland in 1938. Regauged from Huddersfield's unusual gauge of 4ft 7¾in to standard gauge, the trams were numbered 29-36 in Sunderland. Also seen at Seaburn — Sunderland's last tram route — is No 34. Roy Brook

Left:
Sunderland No 24 was one of two trams built in
1933 in the Corporation's own workshops with
bodies that incorporated the bodies from two
trams acquired from Mansfield & District at the
price of £45 each. The two were fitted with EMB
Hornless trucks. No 24 is seen at Fulwell on
1 October 1954. Roy Brook

Above:
Sunderland's last tram, No 86, waits in
Wheatsheaf depot on 1 October 1954 prior to
carrying out its official duty. No 86 was
constructed in the Corporation's own workshops
in 1932 and fitted with an EMB Hornless truck.
Due to the secrecy involved in its construction,
and because of its speed, No 86 was nicknamed

'The Ghost Tram' when new. It set new
standards for Sunderland's tram fleet —
standards which were pursued in the new trams
built for the town thereafter. Of Sunderland's
fleet only one, the ex-MET prototype Feltham
No 100, was immediately preserved. More
recently the remains of 1900-built No 16 have
been discovered and rescued. Roy Brook

SWANSEA AND MUMBLES

Although the Swansea & Mumbles had a history stretching back to the early years of the 19th century — and proudly regarded itself as the world's oldest passenger carrying railway — it was not until 1929 that the line was electrified. It, thus, became the last wholly new electric tramway to open in the British Isles. To operate the line Brush manufactured 13 106-seat tramcars — the largest electric tramcars in Britain — which were to survive through until the line's closure on 5 January 1960. One of the 13, No 1, makes its way towards Mumbles skirting Swansea Bay. The trams, which often operated in multiple, were fitted with doors on the landward side only. After closure, which could only be achieved by the line's owner (South Wales Transport) obtaining a private act of parliament, one of the trams was sold for preservation and based on the Middleton Railway. Unfortunately vandalism, along with the lack of alternative accommodation, led to the vehicle being scrapped. However, the cab section from one car is retained by Swansea Museum. Geoff Lumb

PRESERVATION
CRICH

Left:
Probably the most modern first-generation tramcar to be built in Britain was Leeds No 602. Built by Charles H. Roe, another of the relatively rare crop of postwar tram builders, and delivered in 1953 in a special purple livery to mark that year's coronation, it was designed in furtherance of an aborted tram subway scheme. By the time it was finally introduced, the decision had been taken to abandon the trams, and No 602 eked out its career on less glorious services. Preserved on withdrawal at Crich, now the home of the National Tramway Museum, the car was an appropriate choice for special decoration to mark the Queen's silver jubilee in 1977.
Peter Waller

CARLTON COLVILLE

Established in the late 1960s, the East Anglian Transport Museum at Carlton Colville is one of the few museums where it is possible to travel on both trams and trolleybuses regularly. The museum collection includes parts from a number of trams from the locality, although none is currently operational. In addition, there are trams from London, Blackpool, Glasgow and now Amsterdam on display. Blackpool No 11, the only surviving 'VAMBAC' single-deck tram converted for the Marton route, is seen at the museum in early 1983. *Michael H. Waller*

BEAMISH

The North of England Open Air Museum has effectively created a typical industrial landscape on a greenfield site between Consett and Gateshead. The museum site is served by an electric tramway and one of the trams regularly used is one of the surviving ex-Sheffield 'Roberts' cars No 513. Like No 510 at Crich, No 513 was originally decorated with commemorative panels to mark the closure of the Sheffield system, but a slightly itinerant life prior to reaching Beamish took its toll and the tram has now been restored as originally painted. It is seen here in April 1984. Michael H. Waller

SEATON

The Seaton Tramway in Devon, built on the trackbed of the closed ex-Southern Railway branch to the coastal town of Seaton, was developed from an earlier miniature tramway at Eastbourne. Construction at Seaton started on the 2ft 9in gauge line in 1970 and the first battery-operated services commenced the following year. Gradually overhead was erected and the line extended to its northern terminus at Colyton. The fleet of trams were all constructed specially for the line, although some reuse parts from tram bodies rescued. Double-deck car No 7 is seen heading north towards Colyton in the summer of 1988.
Alan C. Butcher

DUDLEY

A second open-air industrial museum to feature an operating electric tramway is the Black Country Museum at Dudley. Situated at the heart of a 3ft 6in gauge network, it was inevitable that the museum would adopt a similar gauge. When photographed in May 1987 the line was operated by only Dudley, Stourbridge & District single-deck tram No 5, which was originally built in 1920 at the company's Tividale Works. Further trams, including a double-deck car, are under restoration. *Peter Waller*

HEATON PARK

When the tramways of Manchester were
abandoned the short siding which served the
popular Heaton Park was simply tarred over
and forgotten. After much pressure, work started
to reveal the track in 1976 and the first tram to
operate, appropriately the preserved
Manchester combination car No 765, ran in 1979.
Since the early days the track has been
significantly extended beyond the end of the
siding into the park proper. A number of cars
have operated over the line, including ex-
Blackpool & Fleetwood 'Box Car' No 40 which is
seen at the entrance terminus on 12 June 1988.
Peter Waller.

THE MODERN ERA

TYNE & WEAR

The first of the new generation of rapid transit schemes to reach operation was the Tyne & Wear Metro. Largely built on the track of the former BR suburban network, but with a newly constructed tunnel section through central Newcastle and a new bridge across the Tyne to Gateshead, the first section of the Metro opened in 1980. On 5 January 1986, in appropriately wintry conditions, Metro car No 4083 turns at Pelaw. Peter J. Robinson

DOCKLANDS LIGHT RAILWAY

Designed as part of the government's efforts to regenerate the economy of London's docklands, the Docklands Light Railway was conceived as an automatic people mover. Unfortunately, the dramatic growth in traffic, as the Docklands' dream took effect, and a number of technical problems led to complaints when the first sections opened in 1987. However, a great deal of work, plus the acquisition of new vehicles from BREL in Britain and BN in Belgium have significantly improved the position. One of the 'B90' BN-built stock, No 26, is seen at West India Quay on a working to Bank in early 1992. Brian Morrison

MANCHESTER METROLINK

Opened in early 1992, the Manchester Metrolink project brings modern Light Rail technology to the streets of Britain for the first time. The initial phase, which links Bury and Altrincham (over two ex-British Rail routes) via a street section through central Manchester and, through a branch, provides a direct link between Victoria and Piccadilly stations, was opened progressively during early and mid-1992. One of Firema-built articulated cars No 1026 heads toward Altrincham through Navigation Road station on 18 June 1992. The British Rail route from Stockport to Chester is on the right.
Bob Avery

Right:
Paisley No 68, one of a fleet of 72 inherited by Glasgow in 1923, is seen approaching Wakebridge at Crich on 3 May 1992. Much modified during almost 40 years with Glasgow, the tram was restored to original condition at the Museum. *Peter Waller*

Back cover:
The Llandudno & Colwyn Bay Electric Railway was one of the most popular of tramway operators. Despite efforts to prevent closure, the line finally disappeared in 1956. One of the line's ex-Bournemouth double-deck cars, No 9, is seen in Colwyn Bay during the summer of 1954. *Roy Brook*